Published in the UK by
LITTLE **BLACK**DOG LIMITED
Unit 3 Everdon Park
Heartlands Business Park
Daventry
NN11 8YJ

Telephone   01327 871 777
Facsimile   01327 879 222
E Mail   info@littleblackdogltd.co.uk

CW00686734

ISBN 9781904967033

Printed and bound in the UK by Concept Print

FUN & GAMES FOR THE ELDERLY

The Silvey-Jex Partnership

THE RUDE AWAKENING

LET'S GO INSIDE AND TELL MATRON WE'VE COME OUT.
RETIREMENT HOME
SJ.

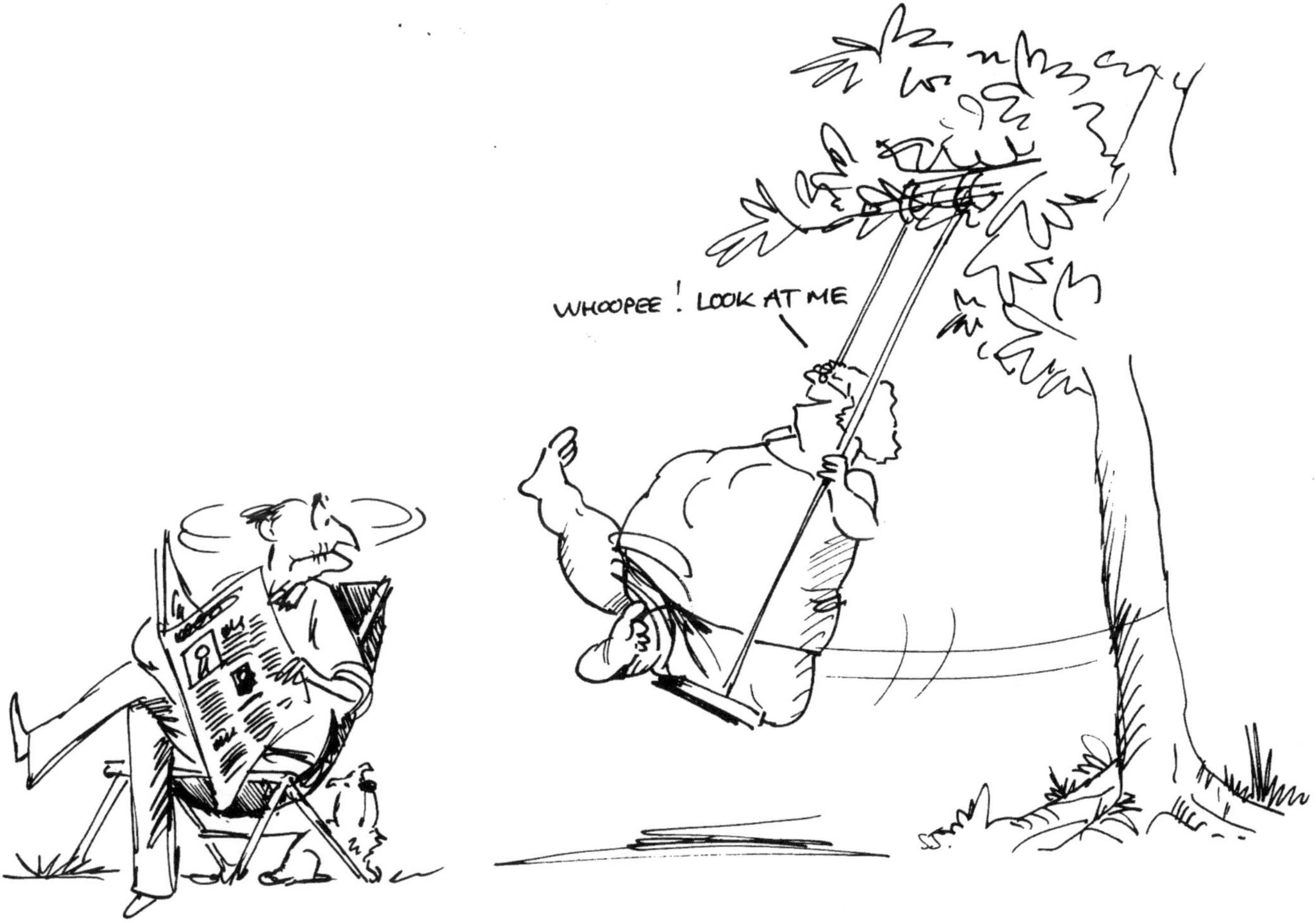
WHOOPEE ! LOOK AT ME

FOR THE LAST TIME ... I'M NOT ENTERING THE VILLAGE WET-T-SHIRT CONTEST
SJ.

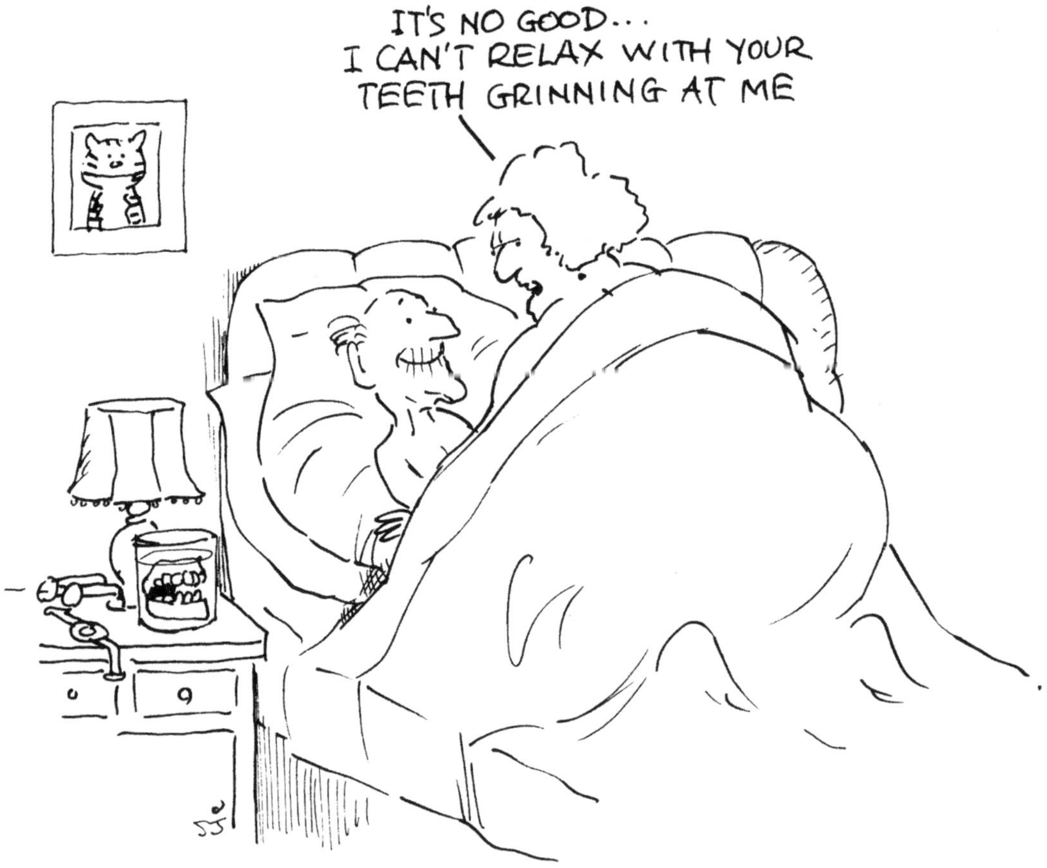
IT'S NO GOOD...
I CAN'T RELAX WITH YOUR TEETH GRINNING AT ME

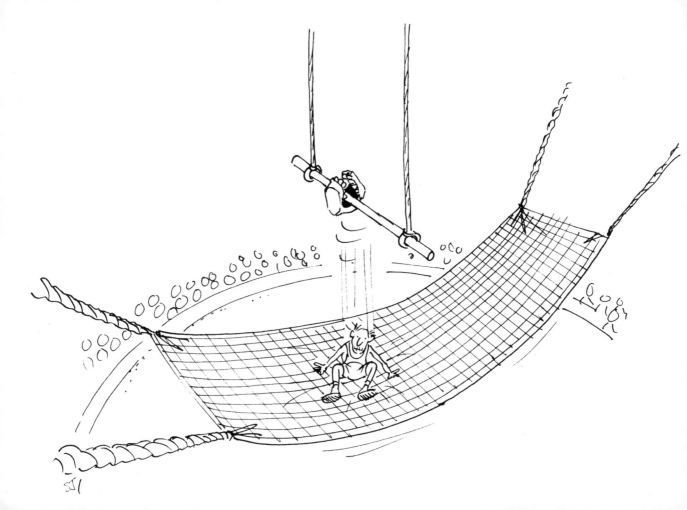

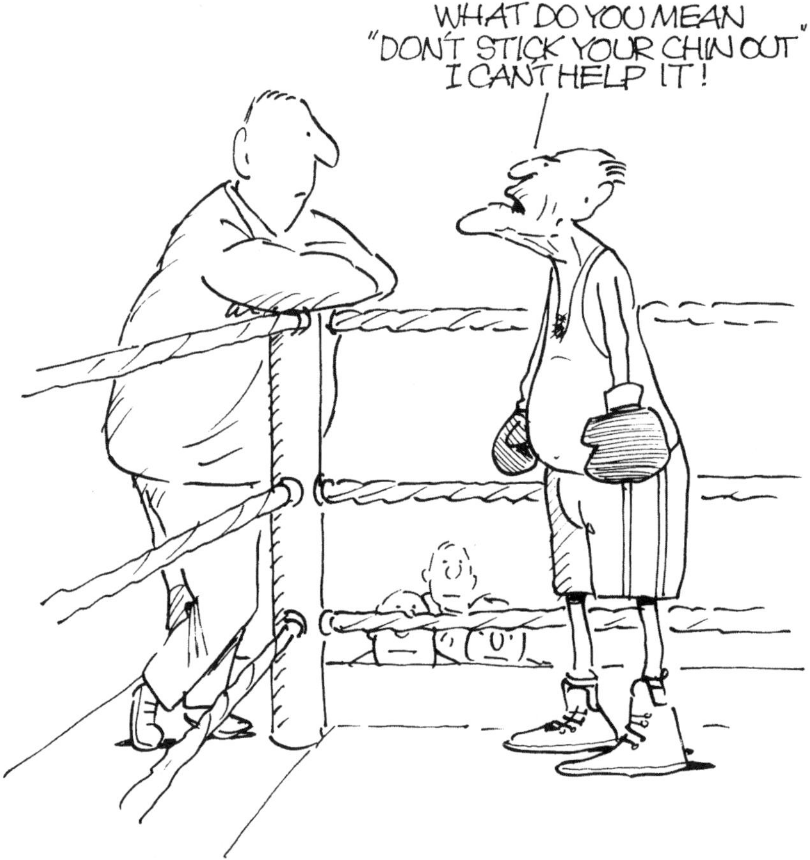
WHAT DO YOU MEAN
"DON'T STICK YOUR CHIN OUT"
I CAN'T HELP IT!

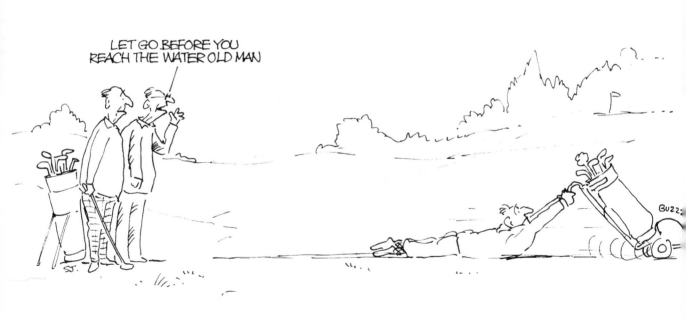

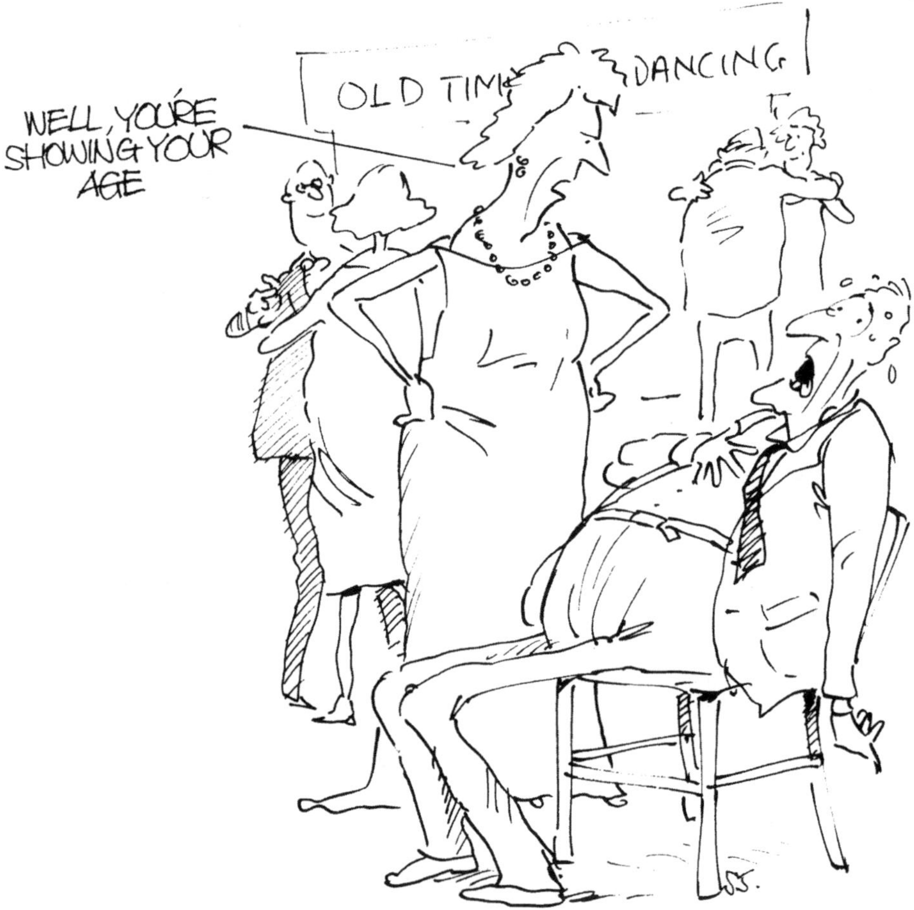
WELL, YOU'RE SHOWING YOUR AGE
OLD TIME DANCING

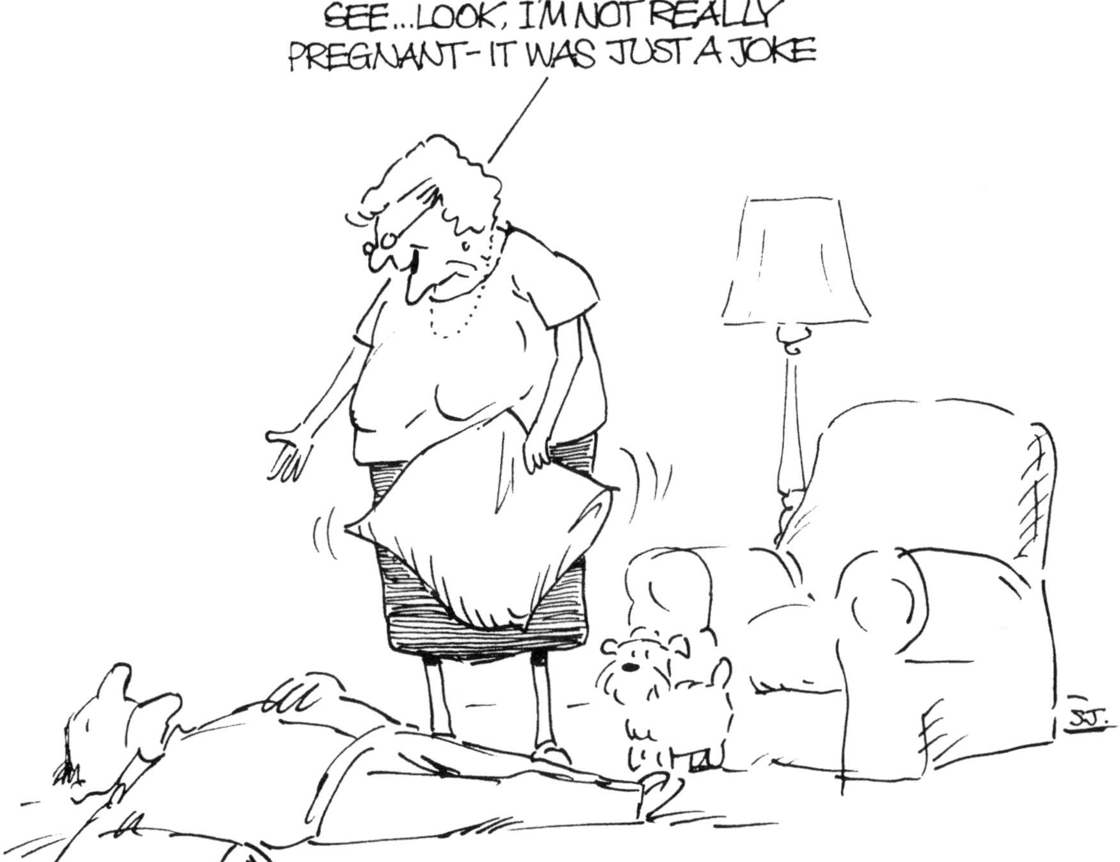
SEE...LOOK; I'M NOT REALLY PREGNANT- IT WAS JUST A JOKE
SJ.

ALLRIGHT... WE'LL SAVE MONEY. YOU IMAGINE YOURE IN TORQUAY. I'LL GO THERE

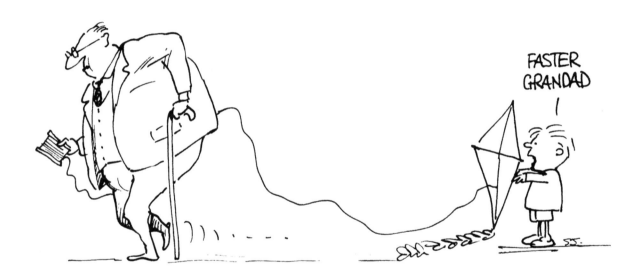